The Ventriloquist

The Ventriloquist

Poems by Charles W. Brice

7.21.2022

WordTech Editions

For Gloria,
I'm throwing my voice to
you! Can you hear me? Are
my lips moving?

All the best,
Charlie

Published by WordTech Editions
P.O. Box 541106
Cincinnati, OH 45254-1106

ISBN: 9781625494078

Poetry Editor: Kevin Walzer
Business Editor: Lori Jareo

Visit us on the web at www.wordtechweb.com

Also by Charles W. Brice:
    Flashcuts Out of Chaos
    Mnemosyne's Hand
    An Accident of Blood
    The Broad Grin of Eternity

Cover art and design by Richard Claraval

For M.L. Liebler

Table of Contents

I

Blazing Crimson Chirper

I hear him before I see him—
    that clipped chirp,
        alluring and inviting.

Once in view I'm captured by
    his flash of blush, fired
        in nature's feathered kiln.

Why name him after the fat princes
    of the church—those money-grubbing
        pretenders to Peter's throne?

Why not call him what he is,
    the Blazing Crimson Chirper,
        whom I greet with my own chirp

when his flight colors my placid yard?
    We converse, we two beings,
        one bewildered, the other beware—

a dialogue of air. Intrigued by
    my imitation of his song,
        he checks me out from

the safety of our bending birch,
    only to fly away, disappointed,
        that I'm not one of his wing there.

Self-Portrait at Seventy

"From my mother's womb untimely ripped," in 1950,
I survived alcoholic parents and smoke-filled rooms,
loved being rocked, "kaka" I called it, not aware of the shit reference—
"Kaka baby?" I asked my mother on an old wire recorder spool;
survived a white blood count that zoomed in 1955
and a heart murmur that put me in the hospital for six months;
twelve years of Catholic education; two bands:
the Rogues and the Kansas City Soul Association—
the drugs, the booze, the brotherhood of music;
the philosophy of Nietzsche, Sartre, and Spinoza that
sent me to my draft board during Vietnam; two years
of conscientious objection at Denver General Hospital—
holding dying hands, back rubs for the terminally ill,
the transfer to the Psych Ward where I met a cute psychiatric
intern from Harvard (how I strained to watch her miniskirt ride up when
she tried to sink an eight ball at the pool table in the Day Room);
the ride up Gold Hill Mountain in Colorado where we were married
by a psychoanalyst masquerading as a minister; the doctor proclaiming,
years later, "It's a boy!" when Ariel flew into our lives;
the thirty-five years that my patients invited me into their worlds
where we laughed and cried together and taught each other how to live;
and now this time of verse, poesy, poetry—the quiet wait
with my Gold Hill girl for that final blister on this path of joy.

Credo

I lost my taste for communion,
too much like cannibalism.
Same for confession: telling
some guy in a dress about
my most intimate indiscretions
seemed an unnecessary humiliation.
Pari Passu, I grew tired
of the robes, the pomp,
the silly servitude.
I lost interest in the goofy music:
They will know we are Christians
by our love, by our love.
I'd never met people so adept
at using "love" to express hate.

Here's what I believe in:
the golden gilded sunrays that
light the sanctuary in the morning.
I want to stand in that light,
in its warmth, inhabit the border
of a holy card, live inside
the egg yolk hues of a halo.

A Stitch in Time

I always loved funerals.
        Cousin Terry died when
I was seven.
        I admired the orchestration
of his disposal
        by the proprietors of
the funeral home in Cheyenne—
        how he was composed
in his coffin, lightly perfumed,
        how intricately a rosary wound
through his cold, wrinkled fingers.

When I was ten, my parents' friend,
        Jack Randolf, died of pneumonia.
"Worked himself to death," my mother said.
        I saw him in his casket,
lifted his head slightly
        when no one was looking.
It was heavy—like winter.

Uncle Francis died when I was twelve.
        The requiem Mass was in a huge
cathedral in Omaha. We gathered
        under a green canopy
at the gravesite while
        rain and tears fell.
The funeral director spread his hands
        in air-embrace and gently
herded us into limousines so
        we wouldn't watch the coffin
slowly lowered into its
        final earthy niche.

My father died when I was fourteen.
        I had a tiny ring embedded
with a fake ruby stone, slipped
        it onto his little finger
when no one was looking.
        Even though fat Auntie Ursal
wondered loudly, as was her way,
        whether it was proper to do so,
my ring is there now on
        what's left of him.

The thread of death and its ceremony
        ties much of my life together,
but not any more than the seams
        of a baseball,
the binding of a book,
        or the helixed hemp
of forty-five years bound
        to the beating heart
of the one I love.

The Cliché That Sunk a Ship

Who heard it first, some hungover Spaniard suddenly awake in a Corunna bordello,
his grip on the sheets softened by the sturdy hands of a señorita?
"The Armada?" he inquired. Her voice serene, "That ship has sailed, mi amor."

Bert introduced me to Coltrane's raging saxophone–scream, rode his Harley
from Omaha to Cheyenne when I was 17 after cutting his wrists
to get out of Viet Nam, knocked

on my door at three a.m. in Denver while on his way to open the first waterbed business
in Chicago, called after his restaurant in Seattle burned down and asked me
to recommend a criminal defense attorney.

Was it Captain Smith's last thought as the North Atlantic engulfed his
wounded vessel, terminally ripped by the iconic iceberg?

Bert invented a gizmo that could have cornered the beverage market
but was too paranoid to let the big companies see the design.

Bert, who got a job during the recession selling Jaguars in Manhattan,
was the top salesman in the dealership until he told his boss to fuck-off.

Maybe the first to utter the phrase was a ten-year-old boy in answer to his mother's
query as to what had become of their floatable craft project that rainy day.

I loved Bert beyond brotherhood but somehow had managed to offend him. I called
and called, but he wouldn't speak to me. Maybe because I told him there was nothing
wrong with putting bread on the table (an awful cliché), when he felt above such things?

Was it the morning Helen realized that the pillow beneath her beautiful head
was more intelligent than her lover? "Send me back to Menelaus," she begged
her dimwitted paramour, to which Paris smirked, "That ship, my dear,
and a thousand like it, has already sailed."

Wherever it came from, whoever first coined that cliché, I used it only once,
when my cousin Bert called after years of silence.

I'd "loaned" him thousands but had never asked for repayment. I only wanted to know what I had done, only wanted to hold onto him a little longer.

Earth orbited the sun twenty-five times without a word from Bert until the night of his call. He hadn't worked for years, mooched off family members who would let him.

That night, after many phony platitudes—flatulent attempts at flattery—he finally launched his spiel: "I think I've come to the end," he said. "My health, my heart, is..."

He wanted money, more money, from me.

"You know that vessel we launched together, the conveyance of our friendship?" I asked him. "Well that ship has sailed," I said, and placed the phone back in its cradle.

Mr. Hippie Meets Dr. Responsible
(A Monologue Disguised as a Dialogue)

You are stuck so in habit:
two cups of tea in the morning,
two Diet Pepsis in the afternoon.

> You think you're so spontaneous
> but look at all the nits you're picking
> with me now. Who cares what I drink?

Have you ever covered yourself with marmalade
and asked passersby to lick it off?

> Of course not, and neither have you.
> As a psychoanalyst I analyzed marmalade lickers;
> I wasn't one of them.

You used to wear a three-piece suit
and tie every day. I bet you practiced
raising your left eyebrow in that analytic stare.

> My analytic stare is ambidextrous,
> and my eyebrows raise themselves quite
> naturally. I never had to practice.

Before you got Ph.D'd you were a lot of fun.
I remember when you spent the summer of '69
naked, a hippie in Butte Canyon, California.

> That macrobiotic diet didn't yin my yang. We
> had to call an ambulance when Marigold, the girl
> who wouldn't eat until she pooped, got constipated.

You were a free spirit, wore sandals and bell-bottoms,
smoked dyna-weed, ate figs dried on a miner's
tin roof in Butte Canyon.

18

The dyna-weed was cut with mescaline
and made me hear screams when
I chomped on those writhing figs.

You were on a tenure track, published fifteen papers, but
walked away from your position at the university.

My colleagues complained relentlessly about
their pitiful lives. I couldn't find an intellectual
conversation in that sea of conformist hypocrisy.

Isn't there anything we can agree on?

You know there is:

We met, and were met by,
the one person who let us be
who we are: Mr. Hippie and Dr. Responsible —

the one who let us be our best, tolerated
our worst, kissed us goodnight, and
hugged us good morning.

Cleaning Up Cat Puke, Naked, at 70

When I was five, I wanted to be a fireman:
point the hose into the blazing window,
save the beautiful lady from a horrible death.

At seven, I gazed upon the waxy but peaceful face
of my dead cousin, a rosary wound through his
fingers just so. I wanted to become a mortician.

The smack of a ball on the end of my bat
sufficed, when I was ten, to set my sights
on a professional baseball career.

At fourteen, the Beatles and James Brown replaced
the blood in my veins and produced kick
beats that made me into a musician.

When I was eighteen, Plato, Nietzsche, and Sartre opened
a world of thought. I planned to pen a philosophy
tome so original there would be no footnotes.

At twenty, I discovered the vagaries of the mind. I became
a psychoanalyst and hoped to write twenty-five
volumes of theory—one more than Freud.

For thirty-five years my patients graciously invited me into
their psyches, but I quit at fifty-five and became a writer,
my most ardent professional love to date.

Today, at seventy, fresh from the shower, I discover a mound
of cat puke on our bedroom floor. Armed with paper
towel and disinfectant, and still naked, I clean it up.

I know, then, that I'm exactly where I belong: naked,
cleaning up cat vomit, at seventy years of age, in the house
where my wife has lived with me for forty-six years,

where we raised our son to become the finest man I know,
where the furry being who produced this putrid
puddle carries no grudges, and neither do I.

P.A.

Sandwiched between an advertisement
for Vitalis and McGregor Corduroy Jackets
an add for "The National Joy Smoke" —
Prince Albert Pipe Tobacco — in the *Pages of Time
Nostalgia Magazine* for the year of my birth: 1950.

A man plays the piano with a pipe in his teeth
while a woman looks adoringly at him:
"Yes," the text reads, "they're in perfect tune.
You can tell by her admiring glance that
he has P.A. (Pipe Appeal)." Twenty-eight years

later I give up cigarettes and turn to a pipe,
but I don't smoke Prince Albert, because
it's cheap and indistinguishable from the
cancer causers I'd abjured. I smoke
Hayward, because it smells like stuffy

offices of literature professors at Oxford, or
how I imagine they smell. Did I have P.A.?
My cardiologist didn't think so. When he smelled
that academic aroma he stood like a Torah
prophet and pointed toward a dumpster.

"Throw that thing out!" Abe Friedman intoned,
channeling his biblical namesake's tormentor.
"Kill your fragrant darling!" I walked to
that nasty dumpster and cast my briared
appendage into the nascent fiery furnace.

At home I told my wife and son that I'd
be crazy, crabby, and cantankerous
for a month. Would they understand?
They did. We three survived my thirty days
in a smokeless desert. I miss my pipe appeal,

especially when I fantasize teaching a group
yearning to be erudite, or merely to place a few words
in the right order. My appeal is reduced to imaginary
patches on the elbows of my corduroy jacket
from McGregor's, stained with Vitalis.

The Book of Friedman

A month away from seventy and I thought I'd understand everything by now because, by seventy, I should have been dead for sixteen years. None of the men on my father's side made it past fifty-four. Why am I the exception? Probably because of my cardiologist, Abe Friedman, who prescribed statins early and Enalapril when my blood pressure revolted in my late forties. For twenty-five years I tried to make Abe laugh but gave up after he asked me, while I was on a treadmill, if I got any exercise. I replied, breathlessly, that "I always make sure to walk from my car on my way into a restaurant." All I got was, "I'm not amused!" He saved my life and didn't want a goodbye card or the flowers I tried to send him when he retired. Maybe I'd understand that if I was dead. Where is it written, in the book of religious fairy tales, that we achieve omniscience after death? Sister Mary Nevertouchyourself taught us that, after death, we wouldn't be interested in seeing our loved ones again, because we'd be in the presence of God. I guess we thought if we were that close to God, we'd acquire his eternal knowledge almost as if we'd become God ourselves which, strangely enough, both Kierkegaard and Joseph Smith believed. Smith claimed that, along with becoming God, we'd get our own planets. Wow! What would I do with my own planet? First, I'd lay in an eternal supply of Diet Wild Cherry Pepsi—wouldn't want to run out of that. I'd make sure my wife and son lived on the planet and that we had baseball and a fine symphony. All the dogs and cats we loved would be there with us along with our friends. We'd write poetry, drink beer, and eat pizza every day. Abe Friedman would be there. He'd check my blood pressure, laugh at my stupid jokes, let me give him flowers and thank him for all he'd done while we were both alive. Oh, and he'd listen to my heart.

Drinks with John

Last night I had a drink in a pub with John Lennon.
 His hair was short and he wore those rimless glasses
  he used to read the world.

We had a nice time although he made fun of the tiny glass
 my drink came in. I'd ordered scotch, neat, and I guess
  in London or Liverpool or wherever we were

they thought that "neat" meant pouring less than an ounce of
 amber goodness into a tiny shot glass
  and serving it to me.

While kidding me he fluttered his eyelids like he did
 in *A Hard Day's Night*. What a delight to hear, once again,
  that Liverpool inflection dipped in honeyed gravel.

He told me many secrets about his time with the Beatles:
 the inside scoop on his relationship with Yoko,
  the dream he had of white space death

that led to the White Album, the story behind "Why
 Don't We Do It in the Road?", some nasty pranks
  he played with Paul when they were young,

his hopes for Sean, what the bullets felt like, where he
 put the strawberries he found in Strawberry Fields,
  but I can't remember any of it.

Was John visiting me from the other world I don't believe in?
 Did he swoop into my dreamscape to let me know
  we'll be having more conversations soon?

In Medias Res

I come from the people whose potatoes went bad,
        whose land had been beaten by English dragoons,
and who had been abandoned by fat boys in Rome—
        some dressed in red and a big one in white.

I come from courage–sweat of firemen in Omaha,
        who spoke in brogues and risked their lives
to save blazing futures, whose wives waited
        in hopeless housedresses for them to come home to

boiled dinners roiling with cabbage, carrots, turnips, salt pork,
        and what meat they could scrounge.

I come from one fireman blown up in a gunpowder factory,
        identified by the scapular wound so tightly round his throat
they had to bury him with it. I come from his great
        grandson, my Uncle Johnny, who so hated dimly lit restaurants that

he would turn on the high beam of a foot-long black police flashlight
        to read the menu and bellow, "This place is too goddamned dark!"

I come from a couple who got lost in a snowstorm
        in Cheyenne, Wyoming, in 1944 and never left.
I come from the prairie—its sweet smell of columbine in summer
        and from the perilous purity of its frozen abyss in winter.

I come from a frayed baseball mitt stained with spit, smelling of leather,
        from a Ludwig oyster pearl drum set with Zildjian cymbals in the basement,

and, in the backyard, from one tulip as red and true as a beating heart.

A Conversation

It was easy enough. I simply reached
into my chest and pulled out my heart,
sat it in a chair, and started in:

"You've given me nothing but trouble," I barked.
"You sit there comfortably today, but for years
you'd surprise me with wild polyrhythms
that no one could dance to."

"Sometimes you act like a convict imprisoned
in my chest, banging on the bars of my sternum —
an *enfant terrible* demanding release. Well
you're out now, how do you like it?"

Bla Blurp Bla Blurp Bla Blurb Bla Blurp.
"Is that all you have to say? Bla Blurp?
Okay, smart ass, I'll find some medical dude
to pinch and poke you with electrodes,

hook you up to an EKG! What's that?"
Bla ha Blurp Bla ha Blurp Bla ha Blurp.
"You think that's funny? Well, I guess
you're right. All an EKG would show

are T waves, troughs, and cardiac impulses
while I want to decipher the depths of your
pulsed scroll, the language locked in pulmonary
veins and atriums. I want to know what's so superior

about a vena cava and what part of the moon
birthed semilunar valves. More than that
I'd like to know why you are so often broken.
Why did you fall for all those losers?

Why do your invisible tendrils encircle
so many dear ones who will soon disappear
down the frail funnel of time?

The Holy Land

Some call it Mecca,
others Jerusalem,
but for me it would be
Liverpool, where four
scruffy guys held
our collective hands
and loved us
yeah, yeah, yeah.

I had a yellow sparkle
Japanese drum kit
my parents bought me.
I learned Ringo's kick beats,
what he liked to do with
the floor tom, the tom tom,
and the high hat: how
he'd set the symbols
so they'd clang together,
produce their own
wall of sound.

I set my ride and crash cymbals
very high, like Ringo,
my stool so high
I almost stood up.
One drunken night
in Wheatland, Wyoming,
my stool broke in
the middle of a solo.
I ran down into the school's
locker room and puked up
the quart of Bali Hai wine
I'd drunk on the eighty-mile
drive from Cheyenne.
Craig, our bass player,
hung me by my collar

from a hook used
for coats in the strong
Wheatland winter.
This was no Cavern Club,
and our band, the Rogues,
remained one of the hundreds
of tiny bands in tiny towns
across the country that went nowhere.
But the Beatles inspired us all,
made us happier with their music,
made our land holy.

The Ventriloquist

At seven I diligently practiced throwing my voice.
My goal in life was to become a ventriloquist
like Edgar Bergen or Paul Winchell. My mother
bought me a Jerry Mahoney dummy so I could
become "the life of the party." That was, according
to her, the best thing that could happen once I grew up.
Jerry and I became pals and often performed for my
parents who wouldn't look at me so that we all
could pretend my lips didn't move.

Then, one summer morning, cousin Terry,
drunk, weary, and battle-scarred, drove his car
into a ditch near Torrington, tumbled front
over end, and crushed his chest—two years
after Korea, finally a casualty of that war.

In the mortuary I felt Terry's cold forehead,
gaped in wonder at the rosary braided
through his wrinkled fingers for eternity.
I watched the mortician gently close
the coffin lid and spread the Stars and Stripes
over his casket—watched him place his hand
over his heart during taps and the marines'
twenty-one-gun salute. He handed me
a spent shell from the firing.

Back home, I found a large box and put Jerry inside.
For three days I prayed for Jerry, wound
a rosary through his wooden hands, felt
the cool grain of his forehead. On the third day
I dug a hole in the backyard and draped
Jerry's cardboard coffin in a tiny flag I'd saved
from the Fourth of July. I cupped my hand and
mimicked a solitary trumpet playing taps and

lowered his coffin into the ground. I threw in the shell
the mortician had given me—imagined marines
giving Jerry a twenty-one-gun salute.

I shoveled dirt over Jerry,
said goodbye,
and caught my own voice,
like a boomerang,
come back to me.

My Face

What about my face? I don't spend time
looking at it, got out of the habit at sixteen
when my face looked like the winner in a
Craters of Mars Lookalike Contest. I spent

so much time scratching my face
that scritch became my theme song
and screech the sound emitted
as horrified humans shrank from me.

And now, an app that finds your twin
in history. Why would I want a twin?
Could the world endure two of me?
For a class project in middle school

our son, Ariel, wrote a report
on General Rosecrans, my great-
great-grandfather. The photo Ari found
of him bore a remarkable resemblance

to me. Rosecrans, a general for the Union Army,
is famous for losing the battle of Chickamauga
in the Civil War. Evidently, he pissed off
General Grant by refusing an order that

would have won the day. Rosecrans,
also known as Rosy, went on to become
a United States Representative from
California. A street bears his name in L.A.

What would great-great-grandpa think
of his maybe not so great great-
grandson—a conscientious objector and
lifelong pacifist? Most likely old

great-great-pap-pap would hop
on his horse, draw his shiny sword,
let out a screech, and ride into
the rosy penumbra of history.

Splainin'

We had front row seats,
mid-ice, $20 apiece, 1985,
Ari's first hockey game.
Lemieux scored his 17th goal
of that season, shot it so hard
he broke the puck. The ref
flipped the biscuit
over the plexiglass—
gave it to us.

That night's promo, a large
plastic thermos, was used by fans
across the ice to beat the puck
out of one another. I distracted
Ari from the melee
by getting him to focus
on the hockey game—
what must have been
a first for the sport!

On our way home we
passed women on street
corners dressed in flimsy
overcoats, wearing thick
red lipstick, looking wanton
as we sped up Fifth Avenue
in Pittsburgh. "Who are those
women?" Ari asked, wide-eyed with
five-year-old wonder. "They are
women of the night," I told him.

Once home, Judy, my sweet
wife and Ari's mother,
asked if we had a good time.
Ari handed her the broken puck
that "Mamoo" had scored, said

the game was fun, but "most
fun of all was seeing the
women of the night."

I had some splainin' to do
that night—oh yeah,
some splainin' to do.

Silence

After the painting by Odilon Redon

Your hush filled the room,
not with criticism, but concern.
Dignified yet vulnerable
your pale countenance covered
Manhattan's burst and blast
with a blanket of quiet.

I visited you at MoMA
at every chance. I imagined
your fingers resting gently
against my lips seconds
before they touched
your own. I suppose

I fell in love with you
a little bit. Last time I
perused those aesthetic
walls, you weren't there.
Your absence a gong
in my heart, sounds of
car horns angry
in my soul.

It's your stillness
I remember—how,
like a shade, you
slipped away even
when you were there.

Degas

How delicate they were:
tutus flared like butterfly wings,
in mid-pirouette,
fingers adjusting a strap,
silky, skillful toes
taut and gliding.

What of that soft female form
entering her bath?
A universe of curve,
the essence of coil,
of swerve,
of arc.

Yet the mind that conceived
each sensual delight,
the eye that envisioned such beauty,
the hands that splashed
image on canvas,
shaped it to clay,

hated an entire people because...
because they shared
the same sky,
the same turf,
a common stage,
the same bathwater.

Congregation Leaving the Reformed Church in Nuenen

After the painting by Vincent Van Gogh

After service they put away
animosity and criticism—
whose topsoil washed away
because he plowed his field poorly,
whose hired man slept
through the storm,
whose cow ran off—

put away at the leaving,
forgiven but not forgotten,
bathed in forest-mist
and barren trees,
in resurrection
and redemption.

They know who they are:
one spiritual body saved,
one divine mass,
congregants together,
plumb with their maker,
lost in heavenly land.

Chagall Room

We call it our Chagall Room because of
the six stained-glass Chagall reproductions,
Christmas presents from Judy over the years,
embedded in the large windows of our porch.

The couch, too, is covered with a blanket
replete with circles, obelisks, rectangles,
floating cows, chickens, kissing couples, and
Menorahs this Russian Jewish master encased

in the blues and crimsons of his dancing heart.
The room glows at dawn with besprent splendor—
spectral hues filtered through these joyous windows.
But when Judy is in the hospital, forced to obey

the tyranny of Crohn's disease, absent from
this room she designed, windows and couch
lose their lively mottles, dissolve into
duns of longing, desire, despair.

That's the way with rooms, isn't it?
The nexus of life we breathe into them
lasts only so long as those inside their
vibrant glory breathe, last, abide.

Musée des Beaux Arts Redux

With thanks to W.H. Auden and Billy Collins

Who dismantled Gauguin's hut and removed
his door, the lintel of which I saw in
1993 at the Musée d'Orsay —
those jolly jambs with the words
Maison du Jouir written on them?

What sensual delight Gauguin took in
the female form, at times *trop jouir* for
his hosts in the Marquesas Islands,
especially Monsignor Martin whose
catechism had captured the callow

on the island and whose lips must have pursed
at the sight of the pornographic photographs
that lined Gauguin's walls. Amid all that
eros, one wonders what *jouir* his children
enjoyed, abandoned as they were in

England. What doors opened for them after
he walked out to pursue his dreams? How rancid
their cakes and ale; how rude the rules they learned
from his absence. What labor performed to
avoid the abyss of *le nom du père.*

The Truth About Stones

It's a wonder Keith is still with us,
that his veins haven't turned to granite.
He and the boys still send satisfaction
from their hearts of stone which
have nothing in common with
rocks resting in the shallows
of Little Traverse Bay,
magnified by rippling tides,
punctuated by the occasional trout
or wide-mouth bass. The gems
of the region, Petoskey stones,
dapple beaches of the Great Lakes
as well as our sandy patch on
Walloon Lake—earthy nuggets,
decorated by fossilized coral,
latticed by the Pleistocene
350 million years ago.
We use a huge one for
a doorstop at our cabin.
And then there are the sandstones
collected by our friend Joyce
on a walk at Sturgeon Bay,
brought back to our place
and stacked by this artist/poet,
largest on the bottom,
smallest on the top,
like tasty beige rockcakes
from a Devonian oven,
arranged and rearranged
for years by Judy and me
according to our joyful
or melancholic vapors.
What will we do with those

lovely layers now that we will
sell our place, leave the watery
womb that held us at Walloon,
we thought, forever?

After Day

After Fin de la Jornada *by Emilio Boggio*

They march alone/together
in the dark,
a scumble of humanity
wet with reality
after a day of
heartbreaking labor
on loading docks,
amid raked dust
of horse stalls
and cartwheeled clicks
on cobbled roads,
a haul of coal,
toward the gleam
of hearth,
an earthy stew,
a fresh loaf,
stories near the stove,
a book read under
sepia candle
or kerosene glow —
harnessed in many ways,
free in others.

Launched in Light

1.

Every morning I open the blinds
as if hoisting the main on a sailboat.
Like wind, a nothing that propels
vessels along waterways, light,
another nothing I can't hold,
or touch, or taste, fills our bedroom—
announces another day on our
beleaguered but still green planet.

2.

People argue over light:
a series of waves,
a gaggle of particles,
waves and particles.
Its contrast with afternoon shadow
heartbeats a room, pushes
particles of my life into
an open-face discovery,
sends waves of warmth
through my biography.

3.

They say that night harbors mystery,
but real mystery is launched in light.
How does something not liquid
pour onto a carpet,
or spread into a room
like a celestial mantilla?
How does a huddle
of vibrating molecules
force a smile or an invisible
wave inspire a song?

Blue Mind

If infinity exists it's
in an ocean gaze—
blue mind,
the scientists call it,
where there's nothing
but water and sky,
where horizon is
a hazy term,
where hope
is unimportant
as is yearning,
sadness, or joy—
even love disappears
into that blurry beyond
of blue mind,
of it's okay,
of Lost is the only
site on the map.

The Sea

Roar that makes the cosmos cower,
waves that carry on their backs
dolphins I aspire to become,
undertow—invisible, sinister, evil,
admirable—takes back what
it gives only to give it again:
treasure of sand and shore,
seashells that echo its voice, green
tangled locks of Aphrodite's hair,
Poseidon's foamy champagne
along its penumbra, aroma
from below, destiny's perfume—
a mist that mimics infinity
and captures eternity's smile.

A Funeral Dance, Walloon Lake, October 2019

Wind hustles leaves alive,
their fall dance, a promenade
of aspen, oak, birch, and beech,
fickle flight through air to ground,
prodigies birthed by death.

Pines, spruce, cedar, and balsam—
wooded elders—watchful as
chaperones, nodding in the gale,
branches slap or clap approval
or angry judgement over

the forest floor blanketed by
a vermeil and umber chorus
where only silence sings and
waits for the soothing
comfort of snow.

Requiem in Winter

The icing lake moves slowly,
pushed by northern Michigan winds,
pallbearers to autumn's corpse—

a somber procession witnessed
by bending spruces, birches,
cedars, and aspens; their sudden

frozen creakings a brutal requiem
with movements entitled
Impermanence, Decay, Endurance.

The Truth About the Universe

Think of it: No space, only a density packed
so tightly it had to explode. Then, like a breasted
body that births purpose and possibility, space
happened, kept expanding to include
everything—all the planets, stars, comets,
asteroids, and us. Space isn't air!
Air is unique to our Goldilocks planet.
We're just the right distance from our sun.
None of this has to do with judgement,
only description, not with gods,
the so-called designers (invented by us
so we can kill people but avoid death
ourselves), invented within that delusion
we call faith, within that cocoon of nonsense
on Saturdays, Sundays, or holy days, that
expands, gets so dense that it, too, explodes,
casting crusaders, true believers, the chosen
to slaughter everyone who doesn't believe
what they believe. Still, the universe continues:
Spins and expands, heaves and hos, without
porridge or green cheese, communion, or
prophet, or interventions from Sky Daddies.
There's nothing that a little gravity
sprinkled with magnetism and
a black hole or two can't do.

III

Naked Athene

Sprung spontaneously from the side
of Zeus's head, Athene was always
a pain in the old man's neck,

and now, out of the choking mist
of tear gas and pepper spray in Portland,
Athene sits on the cool asphalt

of a city wretched and weary and
spreads wide her unclothed limbs
in front of government goons

come to ferry freedom across the river
of forgetfulness. They are stunned,
these camouflaged cowards

with their automatic weapons, their
pitiful pintles posed now at attention,
as if Athene's lovely body of peace

blew for them a lusty/loving reveille,
an anthem that awakens civility
in even the most brutish of bullies.

What He Wants

To hear the boots slapping the pavement
　　　all at once,
see the robotic motions of military hips,
　　　the stiff-armed salute,
heads turned toward the leader,
　　　exhaust-fume parade of tanks,
silent ICBMs, their phallic casements
　　　a "great" death delivery system
measured by thrust.

This is what he wants, what he thinks is power.

What we want is a sunny day,
　　　a place to talk with a friend,
the smell of day lilies and peonies
　　　in the back yard,
the end of open season on our black brothers and sisters,
　　　the rights in the Constitution we're supposed to have
and he's supposed to protect.

Power is an ephemeral creation—
　　　tentative and temporary;
just ask Mussolini and his girlfriend who,
　　　had it not been for the bullet holes,
looked like they were auditioning trapeze artists
　　　for the Greatest Show on Earth.

Driving to Sturgeon Bay After the Massacre in Las Vegas

Drive north on Townsend Road,
the road you love to walk lined with
dogwoods and wilted cornstalks.

> *The sniper's perch was on the 32nd floor.*
> *He fired mercilessly into the crowd*
> *come to listen to country music.*

In Petoskey, turn right on Charlevoix Ave.
then left when you get to Michell St.
Continue on North 31.

> *The sniper brought 23 rifles into his hotel room.*
> *They found another 19 in his home.*
> *Who needs 42 rifles?*

Turn left onto MI-119 and drive to Harbor Springs,
the charming little town with the lovely church.
Take a right, past the post office and continue

on MI-119 into the Tunnel of Trees. Look at
your wife of 45 years. Tell her she looks like she's 40.
Say, "Isn't this beautiful?" as Lake Michigan
peaks through aspen, birch, the beech trees.

> *One young woman didn't like concerts, didn't go*
> *out much, but she loved country music. The sniper*
> *shot her through the head. She was 20 years old.*

MI-119 winds and weaves; sun dapples
the woods, ghosts of trillium and sweet pea
bloom in your memory. Queen Ann's Lace
cushions your drive. Somewhere a heron walks.

One fellow survived Afghanistan, had gone deaf
in one ear from explosions. The sniper shot him
in the chest. He didn't make it. He was 29 years old.

Drive through Good Hart and Cross Village.
On the radio listen to a lady who was trapped
with some severely wounded people.

My sister said I was meant to be there;
to hold them as they died.

When you get to Sturgeon Bay help Judy
traverse the dunes in her walker. Let Mugsi
off her leash. Watch her run. Kiss your wife.
Listen to the waves.

On Gratitude

Judy and I watch videos of Billy Collins reading
poetry and use them to prompt our own writing.
We're lucky to be writing poetry in our dotage.

We were, for years, two shrinks. She hates it
when I tell people that she, a psychiatrist, drugged
her patients while I, a psychologist, got them over it.

We show our poems to each other, critique them,
make suggestions, make them better.

Today we watch Billy read poems by African American poets—
a video recording made a month ago on Juneteenth,
but today is July 19, 2020, the day after John Lewis
died from pancreatic cancer, probably the only malevolence
he suffered in his long life that wasn't racist.

John Lewis faced down batons of hate on Edmund Pettus Bridge,
led a sit-in on the floor of the House of Representatives
to rid our country of its rabid gun habit,

was arrested forty times over the years for claiming
that he was a human being with rights, and was,
to the end, optimistic that one day, in our country,
every one of us would be free.

I'm grateful for Billy Collins who shares himself, his work,
and the poems of others during this COVID nightmare,
giving us something that hallows our every day.

I'm grateful for this lovely woman with whom I live,
for her lyrical poems, her helpful hints about my work,
and her steady presence in my life.

I'm grateful for John Lewis, whose life of courage
makes two old white people, poets in Pittsburgh,
feel privileged to inhabit the same earth as did he.

Las Vegas

After reading The Irrelevance of Power *by Frank Seeburger*

I've never been there but
I don't need to go—I'm
always already there.
Our country has become Las Vegas.
Cacophony of slots and roulettes makes
thought impossible. A mephitic mix
of smoke and pure oxygen renders
breathing an economy of gasps and coughs.
News blares twenty-four hours a day,
for everyone, for no one.
We are all a flat screen.
Neon commits larceny
on the spectrum,
embezzles the color wheel,
turns green into glitz,
dyes with dolor
the fabric of humanity.
Fifty yards of gluttony
makes a buffet—
breakfast, lunch, dinner
and desserts brought to you
by sugar barons and GMOs.
Desserts in the desert
that consume your
undead corpse.
You are a cigarette
with a mouth attached,
a cocktail that grew fingers,
a sweaty sex organ dripping
with desire, unremitting,
unrequited—where love
never made it to the strip,
but hid, still hides, underneath
a desk in middle school.

In this country Zeno's arrow
never leaves his quiver. Here
Clemence convinces himself
he never heard the splash,
and cop after cop walk
past a bleeding man
they pushed to the ground
because he wanted to stop them
from killing black people.
What a gamble! We've cashed in
our chips, received nothing
on our returns. Every four years
we look for a clearing
that would let us see the forest
and the sky. But we pave it over
as soon as we find it. Las Vegas
abhors a vacuum. In 2016
we needed FDR. Instead,
we got P.T. Barnum.
The house always wins.

Blackbird

A knee broke
the blackbird's neck
but now knees contract
in contrition and
street curbs weep.

Broken, he flies over
400 years of stay put,
400 years of moneychangers
desecrating our country
with his people's chains;
he flies over hate, shame, division,
across the demesne of white privilege,
to bring us day, sun, warmth—
change.

His midnight song is gone.
Like MLK he won't
get there with us,
but he leads us
to the far side
of freedom,
to the soul missing
from the cop's shoe.

The eye of a needle is small.
George Floyd threads it for us all,
threads it still,
for some things
you can't kill.

Vietnam Again

We sat for hours in my car,
a baby blue Mercury Comet,
in the alley behind Owen's house
in Cheyenne, 1968. He was
gonna enlist the next day. We'd

served Mass together, drank
crazy like high school kids,
played baseball on
different teams—always
buddies no matter the score—

double dated, whispered the
secrets of grasping, awkward,
adolescent love to one another.
He'd been voted *Most Handsome,*
Most Likely to Succeed.

You'll be trained to kill, I argued.
I know you. You can't do that.
You'll become another disposable
particle of LBJ's ego. Vietnam's
an illegal, immoral war. You
can't go, I almost pleaded—
no, I pleaded.

It's the right thing to do, he said,
besides, I've had it with school.
The army will make me a man.
We went back and forth until
our night of Coors quarts turned
into a dry-tongued dawn. The

fingerposts of our futures diverged
wildly: I returned to college and
applied for conscientious objection.

Owen signed the papers held
in the recruiter's hands.

Six months later I leaned into
the gelid Laramie wind, opened
the envelope from my draft board
that could portend five years in prison
or a life of exile over our northern border, but
my plea against killing had been accepted!

I fell into a fever worthy of a Russian novel:
roiling in my sheets, floridly hallucinating,
stranger to dream and reality alike, when
Owen appeared at my door. He'd gone to
bootcamp where they'd taught him to scream
"Die Gook!" while he practiced gutting
a human being with a bayonet.

He couldn't take it. When they wouldn't
allow him to file for conscientious objection
he simply left, went AWOL. He'd landed
on my doorstep on his way to Canada—
a fugitive I was happy to harbor.

He's alone now, high all the time,
never married, no children,
angry and disillusioned,
an out-of-work social worker
in Casper. But in my mindscape
we're back in that car,

a comet in the sky,
behind his house, on
a frosty night in Cheyenne,
midwinter,
mid-war,
mid-America,
mid-hope.

Prayer in the Time of Coronavirus

Praying to God about COVID-19
is like asking a fox
to lay an egg
after he's eaten
all the chickens.

The Divine Image

After William Blake

This old atheist reads William Blake
and finds in each act of kindness
the divine revealed.

Doctors, nurses, ward clerks, receptionists
meet the sick in emergency rooms and
wonder if the one they'll care for

will kill them. They wrap their woe and
worry in bandages of love, masks
of care and concern,

pump chests that harbor
an invisible death, reuse
aprons and paper suits,

ride the bus—a petri dish of disease—
to work, wash hands raw,
sleep on their feet,

drop their clothes in foyers
and vestibules so their kids
and partners won't get sick.

Redemption floats in this world
and above this world. Divinity
abounds in the faces of these

men and women where pity finds
its form in mercy and peace and
in the beating hearts of all.

Bottled Lives

We're living in a laboratory beaker.
> *No restaurants*
> *No coffee shops*
> *Avoid everyone by six feet*
> *Stay in the house*
> *The backyard's okay*
> *Walk outside away from people*

Words emailed to our friends
from their daughter,
an infectious disease physician.

Judy, my sweet wife,
riddled with arthritis,
pinned and prodded
by a ruptured disk, prepares
medical marijuana squares
garnished with cream cheese
and brown sugar.

I make my world-famous social-
distancing chicken noodle soup
(in my apocalyptic panic
I forget the noodles!)
and my quarantine-special yellow cake
with homemade chocolate frosting.

We sit in our porch room,
listen to Chopin,
write poems,
and marvel at how
shadow and light prism
through our lives.

Like bees captured in a jar
we buzz around,
bump into glass walls,
dream of the world outside.

New Vows

I promise to stand six feet away from you
during our wedding ceremony.

I promise to brush, floss, and gargle with mouthwash
before and after I kiss you.

I will scrub all my essential body parts with antibacterial soap
before we make love.

I pledge to wear sterile disposable rubber gloves
when I caress you.

I vow to chant William Blake's poem, "How Sweet I Roam'd
from Field to Field" three times every time I wash my hands.

I will now, and forever more, cough into my arm
when in your presence.

I will never, ever, pick my nose again.

I swear to quarantine with you beyond grey hair,
illness, and fear.

I will hold you in arms you cannot see,

recognize your forgiving smile no matter
what mask you wear,

search past lash and lid for the resplendence of your eyes,

and cherish you in contagion's fire until my fevered
chest heaves its last.

After COVID Is Over

I'll go to the library more. I miss
the smell of paper, print, dust,
and mouldering paste assembled

by careful and caring fingers or
indifferent machines to preserve
conversations of the ages.

I'll go out to eat less than I used to,
but I'll enjoy it more—carefully read
the menu, ask the wait staff details

about what spices were used, whether
the chef prefers butter or margarine,
that sort of thing. Mostly, though,

I'll look across the table at friends
we invited to eat with us. We'll
laugh at their jokes and fuss over

their insights into literature, politics,
movies, or how to properly care
for the orchids we bought at grocery stores.

We'll open our mouths wide to savor
each morsel of food and opinion and not
fear the spread of anything beyond ideas,
succulent delights, and good cheer.

COVID Dispatch

I sit in my porch room,
a rainy day in Pittsburgh,
and listen to Khachaturian's
Gayaneh Ballet. I ignore
the lively, playful parts, listen
only for yearning and strife.

I absorb melancholy and think about
sandhill cranes on Walloon Lake.
I miss their prehistoric banter, their legs
dragging behind them in flight like
retracted landing gear, their prayerful
umber glimmer at sunset.

At almost seventy, my hands covered
with age spots, having cut my face
with scissors this morning while
trimming my shaggy gray beard, and
feeling in my limbs that one day
I won't be able to rise unassisted
from a chair, I learn that our COVID
quarantine will last for thirty-six months.

I think about sandhill cranes.
We all fly south, but into the
winter, not away from it.

The Altered Eye

For the Eye altering alters all...
William Blake

Last year my friend Steve was sick.
The hounds of his heart ran wild
in his chest and ate their fill, until
his doctors finally collared them
too late to undo their ravage.

He was housebound for a year,
had to stay home away from
dandelion and sunflower,
rose and churchyard—all
manner of floating infectors.

Now the world is sick, and Steve
stays home like the rest of us,
quarantined against invisible intruders, but
unlike last year, ringed by wife and kids.
"It's the least isolated I've been in a year,"
he writes, and alters the landscape,
the inscape—alters all.

Waiting Room Again

The lady with three kids
in the corner of the room yells:
"You want your ass warm?
I'll beat your ass in front of anyone.
Don't think I won't!" She
screams as much for us
as for her doomed offspring.
This fleshy prodigy–producer
should have taken a Do Not Reproduce
pledge, but no luck. "I'll beat your ass,"
she bawls again, and I find us another
place to sit, far away from this
impresario of abuse.

Judy has to get another injection
for the relentless pain in her hips and back.
Her cane keeps a mordant rhythm while
we move to our new seats only to hear
the lady in the wheelchair by the fish tank
loudly proclaim, "What matters
is that you're saved. The water
doesn't mean a thing. You're saved
what's important!"

They take Judy for her injection, and
I jam plastic buds into my ear canals,
hoping that Khachaturian will save me
from wailing fanatics and frantic,
ferocious Medusas. When Judy returns
we go to lunch at the Regent Square Café.
I have bacon and eggs, she French toast.
The injection doesn't work, her pain returns,
but the food is good, and the drive back
made marvelous by the green/yellow gleam
of sycamores that line our route home.

The Impossible Profession

A friend's therapist tells him that he shouldn't get married
unless he's ready to be alone. Oh, the damage my
well-intentioned former profession has done.

If you're ready be alone,
    be alone.
If you're ready to get married,
    find someone with whom you want
to travel this dusty road,
    a thou who will transform your I
from an ephemeral ego into a vision
    of the other person.
Find someone who is your Everest, your Grand Canyon,
    your Milky Way.

How much does the Earth weigh?
What a silly question. It floats
out in space like the rest of us. Still,
scientists claim it weighs 1.3×10^{25} pounds or
13,000,000,000,000,000,000,000,000 pounds!

Should we put Earth on a diet?
Shrink it to a more manageable size?
Or should we leave it alone? Let Earth be Earth?
"What is, is, and what is not, is not," proclaimed Parmenides,
which gets me back to my friend's therapist:

He must see the Earth as a huge, swirling, bulbous, graveyard
where, as Jim Morrison wrote, "No one here gets out alive,"
and Jim should have known since he died from his excesses at twenty-seven.
Still, to use a term from my psychoanalyst past: to prepare
for death on your wedding day is a bit counter-phobic.

You can see the earth as a huge dirt clod that explodes against the wall of time,
or you can view the earth as a world—a nexus of possibilities
that allows a seedpod planted in the soul of the cosmos
to blossom into a relationship, into the one that makes two possible.

Poet Framed by Snow

For Jason Baldinger

On the hottest day in June,
91 degrees in Pittsburgh, Jason
posts a photo of a trip to Montana
taken one year before this
molten moment in Iron City.

In the photo he wears
a stocking cap, a tarn
behind him framed by
snow-draped mountains.

He'll warm up, I think.
All he needs is a
glass of crisp hooch,
campfire-stoked embers,
and a few words on paper
from his poet's pen—
words that make each
heartbeat count,
that coat with comfort
the endless chain of
meaningless jobs,
the absurd labor of
the many he writes about:
the broken backs,
the broken lives.

Clarity

I write my friend Jerry to ask
if he'll join me in a Zoom poetry reading.
He's busy writing essays these days,
he replies, and will get back to me

"whenever clarity comes around again."
If it's Clarity he awaits, it could be years
before I hear from him. At seventy, I think Clarity
has lost my address—maybe not a bad thing.

As an altar boy in Cheyenne in the sixties, Clarity's
avatar was a young priest, Father Coherence,
who insisted that we fold our hands in prayer
when not handling cruets of wine and water,

the holy water boat, or the censer whose
sacred contrails perfumed the heavens.
We had to cross our thumbs over one another,
so that even those pudgy digits bodied-forth

our Savior's bloody sacrifice. In 1968, in Father
Coherence's religion class at St. Mary's, Clarity
made me wait until he'd passed out all the final exams.
Mine was last because I'd answered all the questions

perfectly—the only member of my class to get 100%.
Clarity dropped by again today while I searched
the internet for Father Coherence and found there
his shadow: arrested in 1995 for public lewdness

(he'd used his fleshy aspergillum to "bless" a coat
sleeve hanging on a rack) and, to broaden the space
of the dis-grace, accusations of molestation by
three adolescent boys between 1984 and 2003.

And so, I offer a prayer for my friend Jerry:
May Clarity be for you a restless relative,
one you love, have to put up with when he
visits, but doesn't stick around for long.

He Was No Urthona[1]

We called him Ed the talking horse.
He was so important to himself,
this man in the closet with a cassock.
"You can't do it unless you
imagine it first," he'd insist—
his bombast that of a fascist.
We almost yawned to death.
Every faculty meeting:
"The imagination is primary!"

Tell it to Pierre as he runs for the bus,
I wanted to yell, referencing Sartre
who actually wrote a book
on the imagination. *Don't you know
that your ego only exists once you've
already done something?* I wanted
to say, but never did. I was a lowly
assistant professor who looked forward
to these faculty meetings in the way
an inmate might anticipate his next
serving of oatmeal.

Requiem for the Future of the Past

Head sinks into pillow,
eyes shut,
the dream begins:
inside a haze of images,
the dead come alive again.

At St. Mary's High,
in the auditorium
where we escape the nuns,
a group of boys, my friends,
and in their midst Paul Visca,
thin and athletic,
hair neatly combed,
a sly smile parting his lips.

I want to tell him that,
if he doesn't love more carefully,
find a woman who won't leave,
he'll wake up one morning
forty years from now
alone in a mountain home
in Colorado,
try to get dressed,
but die instead.

I want to cry.
He won't understand
my knowledge of the future.
I force a hollow grin,
give a little wave —
of hello,
of goodbye.

Slyboots

I thought she had a rollicking,
if indecorous, sense of humor.

In the gym she was a double-wide
in a sea of lean. On the treadmill

next to me she described the blowjob
she'd provide if only I'd succumb.

She was oblivious of her husband, whom
I liked, and my wife, whom I loved.

She reminded me of Cordelia, the brainless
babe on Buffy the Vampire Slayer who

thought that Marie Antoinette got a raw
deal since she served her people cake. My

blowy buddy had a son, ten years old, willful,
energetic, curious, whom she ignored

during seductions. She promised, one night,
to read him a story if he went to bed. Once

he pulled the covers under his chin, she reneged.
"Too tired," she said. "Your mother's very smart,"

the father told the son. "You should know better
than to trust her." The two, husband and wife,

laughed while the boy wept in outrage. Today,
ten years later, I read in the paper that

the son has masterminded a fraudulent scheme.
He's being arraigned as the apple who,

while fallen, is still attached to the tree.

Relationship Haiku

He only saw the "I"
not the "we." One cup
in the cupboard.

Mother held him when
it was convenient.
Nostalgia.

Forty-five years together.
Who cares where
you put my iPod?

Upset because we argue?
Quiet! Listen to
the grave's caress.

Sonnet for Camus

A poet keeps time with his heart,
a metaphor maker, hardly a pump,
that lets church bells sing
and freedom ring, or not.

Time can't be found in a clock.
Our world is more than a rock.
Youth exists in the mind
unbound by logic that limps behind

how we really live in our turbulent times,
where love is the shortest second of all
and so many, day to day, live with gall
and weary toward death in a dreary line.

We push, stumble, and fall
and, like Sisyphus, we climb.

Leftovers

> *After the scavengers are gone,*
> *the white skull laughs.*
> David Baker

Everyone has to eat.
The California Condor almost went extinct.
Wasn't there enough death to go around?
That last morsel lodged inside

an empty eye socket is delectable—
reminiscent of brown bits scraped
out of a frying pan while plating
pork chops in rosemary vinegar reduction.

It's always what's last that delights.
After all the hurrahs and laments
someone makes coffee
sits down

takes a sip
waits for sunrise.

What's Remarkable

All those stories about people who think
This is it, but it isn't. The plane doesn't crash,
the chest pain abates, the hoarse voice and
dry cough is just a cold. There's the bloom
of spring: the serviceberry tree looks like
a huge albino peacock trying to impress
a lady bird, peonies that sway hello
in summer's subtle breeze, what
afternoon sun does to your porch floor.
There's your dog who knows exactly where
she likes to be scratched and presents
her heinie in gleeful expectation. There's
pork chops in rosemary vinegar reduction,
and the feel of your wife's cheek in
the middle of the night.

Then there's when *This is it* is it.
No one reads that story which is stored
in the abyss, in the space between spaces,
in the White Hotel that has no rooms.

The Truth About Finitude

Time stands next
to my bookshelf,
lips curled against
decay's sweet aroma. He
looks at his watch,
taps his foot
impatiently,
like a tired tercel
pecks the last
of his kill.

"You're always late,"
he says, "and you'll never
read all those books."

Les Mouches

Love or hatred calls for self-surrender.
J.P. Sartre, The Flies

He liked to keep it wet and warm—no matter
that *l'autre femme* shot drugs through her veins,
no matter how often he carried their *mauvaise foi*
back to Faith and their marital bed.

He told Faith, only a few months earlier,
that he wanted to die holding her hand
then trashed their room; torched their playhouse.
"We should never have been together!"

"It wasn't sex," he said, his head tilted like
the dog on the old RCA Victor record label.
I thought about his dying fingers braided
with Faith's, a simulacrum, now, of flies.

"Everyone has a dark side." He wanted my
understanding, that impotent unction of our
therapeutic age. Instead, we stood in a coffee
house, shook hands, and said goodbye.

My hand remembered resting on a coffin's
lid a few years back, its metallic surface
a poor substitute for flesh, and today,
in his hand, *un autre décès*.

92

The Mirror Stage

Identity didn't exist in the fourteenth century.[2]
Nobody wondered who they were—
they knew: either they were peasants
who spent their lives working for others,
making babies, and waiting to die, or

they were the noble class who spent
their time waging war, making babies,
and waiting to die, so they could pass
on their possessions and reap their
just reward in the next life.

So what is this carapace we crawl inside,
carry wherever we go; this Self, invented
by psychoanalysts, that we constantly
cultivate and that gets in between
ourselves and others all the time

but random images reflected to us by
parents, siblings, teachers, friends—
fellow travelers in this veil of years?
Some of us wear fedoras and payot,
others prune and preen in imitation of

their avatars in the pages of Vogue or GQ.
Some wear T-shirts in winter, others gray
government suits, blue shirts, red ties,
ready for their television appearances.
Some are captured in nearly invisible

bikinis, swim trunks, and flat stomachs
cavorting with the terminally happy
in places like Spice Island, Casa de Campo,
and Belmond La Samanna. We are obsessed,
in our confusing and divided times,

not so much with graven images of old,
but with a modern excarnation: The Self
reflecting on itself. Shipwrecked on Illusion
Island, we worship ourselves, our craven images,
gravid with death and gravebound.

Four Haiku

At night in bed my dreams
hide behind a glass
of cold water.

My sweet wife is
seventy-five years old.
Raindrops splatter the skylight.

We sold our lake cabin.
The Milky Way,
a blended blur of light.

Gnarled fingers struggle
to twist the jar lid.
A lily lives just a day.

You Opened the Door

In memory of Jim Harrison

You opened the door wearing only your boxer shorts
and asked if I knew who I was. Of course not, I said.
You asked if I lived in a gated community.
Only spiritually, I said, and we became friends.

You asked if I knew who I was. Of course not, I said.
I was worried: many of your characters drowned themselves.
You asked if I lived in a gated community.
You were no longer suicidal, you said.

I was worried: many of your characters drowned themselves.
You told your uncles you were going to major in English.
You were no longer suicidal, you said.
Everyone knows fuckin' English! one of your uncles said.

You told your uncles you were going to major in English.
You asked if I lived in a gated community.
Everyone knows fuckin' English! one of your uncles said.
You opened the door wearing only your boxer shorts.

Towed

The sign reads *Patient Parking Only—All Others Will Be Towed*.
I feel sorry for them already—the towed non-patients who thought
they'd make a quick run into a local store.

Maybe they encounter a friend, or have trouble finding an item,
or simply become preoccupied with the largesse of capitalism
in the early twenty-first century.

Return to the parking lot occasions momentous disorientation, the kind
Icarus experienced a second before he realized Daddy was right:

> Where's my car?
> Is this the right lot? .
> There's a space where my van used to be!
> Who took my truck?

Then commences the one-foot-over-the-other stagger also known as
the Boogie of Bewilderment. Soon shame covers the non-patient like
steamy asphalt poured onto a naked street's sub-base. Recovery

from shame entails the kicking of the ether, the fist-clenched punch
of the nothing that is. Rage wanes when nothing acts like nothing and
fails to punch back, producing enormous ego-deflation that opens

onto the worst humiliation of all: punching in a phone number for a spouse,
sibling, friend, or even grown child who will drive the non-patient
to the junkyard and try not to laugh, scowl, or scold.

Instructions for Golfers

First, wash your balls! To play the game
with dirty balls is to dishonor it. Then place
a ball on a stick that's flat on one end and
jam it into the sward. Grab a club that has

a big block of wood on its end and grip it
as if you are ten years old and making
a secret handshake with a friend. Now,
wiggle your heinie like you would if

a swarm of fire ants jumped into your pants
and began to omnivore your privates. Gaze
down the fairway at a tiny flag on the
horizon—squint and aim for it.

Whack the gleaming ball and watch its
antiseptic flight into the ether as birds,
bugs, foul, and all legitimate nature
avoid its rude trajectory. Hop into your

motorized wain and pretend, over the roar
of the engine, that you are both engaging
nature and exercising in it. Breathe deeply
the gaseous air and smirk at your comrades

as their carts crisscross what was once a
placid grassy plain. Congratulate yourself
on the masculine dismount from your chariot
as you make the heroic decision about

which club to use for your approach shot. Oh
the tension as you survey the 3 iron, the 5 iron,
and choose, with trembling hand, the 7 iron.
Wiggle your keister again as you prepare

to abuse the grass-besmirched orb that, only
moments ago, you so gently bathed. With
the courage of Custer at his last stand, watch
the ball bounce toward the tiny flagpole

on the green. Look down and notice
you've uprooted a six-inch swath of turf.
Grab a clump of dead flora and further molest
it with your cleated shoe— tell yourself you've

healed a cosmic scar. Return to your cart, open
the cooler in the back, and pop the top on a cold one.
Marvel at the mix of fermented cattle feed that slithers
down your throat at only half past eight this morn.

Nature is grand, you think on your way to the
matted surface of chemically stunted grass you
call *the green.* Crouch down, and extend your
putter from your crotch toward the hole. It's so long!

Imagine your ball as it travels the slope and curve
of the soft sod and sinks deep into the abyss. Stroke
your ball. You love to stroke your ball. Watch it
meander toward the hole, kiss its lip, but fail to enter

its sanctum sanctorum. No matter, only a quick spurt
from your putter and poof, your ball disappears into
that tiny dark continent. Sigh with satisfaction, wipe
your brow, and repeat these steps seventeen more times.

Once home, refuse your wife's demand that you
shower before entering her boudoir, certain that her
amorous reluctance will willingly succumb to the
manly musk that pulsates from your virile visage.

St. Rose of Lima

She was an occasion of sin. Men would see her,
and their apostate gushers would fill holy water
fonts from Pisco to Puno, Lisbon to Pucallpa.
The entire male population of Peru teetered
on the edge of Hades, and she knew it. Her parents
wanted her to marry, be merry, act like a normal girl,
but Rose had different ideas. What about those
poor backsliders enraptured by her silky dark hair
and smooth olive skin? Because of her irresistible
beauty, so many souls sizzled, sputtered, bubbled up

in Satan's skillet that his stupendous spatula couldn't
handle all that spiritual bacon. To stop the drooling
and dripping, Rose cut off her hair, slathered her face
with hot peppers until it blistered, and placed a homemade
crown of thorns on her head. But wait, that wasn't enough
to atone for the shameful venery caused by her gorgeousness.
She was an expert seamstress and regularly took a sewing
needle and plunged it deep into her scalp, probably
penetrating her brain. No wonder she had visions
of the Devil. Since she was a saint-in-waiting she evidently

didn't have to worry about infection. Guess pre-canonization
was the seventeenth century version of antibiotics. Well, maybe not;
she died at thirty-one. I only read three books at St. Mary's Grade School:
St. Rose of Lima, Blessed Martin de Porres, and the Lou Gehrig story.
I wanted to give away all my clothes to the poor, like Blessed
Martin, but my parents didn't take to that idea, and I certainly
wasn't up for sticking a pin in my head (besides, I wasn't, as
far as I knew, an occasion of sin—but maybe perusal of some
priestly diaries might prove otherwise). So, I chose baseball.
I'm still a follower of St. Lou.

My Life in Oatmeal or Bla Bla Bla

Five years old and in Memorial
        Hospital, 1955, Cheyenne, Wyoming.
They always burned the oatmeal.
        Its acrid smell announced five a.m. —
the beginning of each day. Finally
        discharged after five months with

a diagnosis of "possible rheumatic fever,"
        my life had no oatmeal in it for years.
I never fixed it myself until the late seventies
        when, overweight, I went
on the Pritikin Diet. He was big
        on oatmeal and all things

vegetarian and oil-less. After a while
        I thought I heard myself squeak
when I raised a limb, so oil free was I.
        I learned to make oatmeal, slice
half a banana, and pour skim milk
        over the fruit and the steamy surface.

The smell of unburnt oatmeal is lovely —
        like the odor of the paper
in your favorite novel. I dropped
        fifty pounds thanks to Pritikin
but put it all back on once my sweet
        wife rightly declared that

my entire diet tasted like a mixture of
        liquid cardboard and solid cardboard.
Liberated, I went back to eating steak,
        chips, cheese, and gobs of food
with all the oil in it I could find.
        In the nineties I had to fashion

a new wardrobe: my "jumbo line,"
        my sweet wife called it. This development
necessitated a commitment to Weight Watchers
        where I learned a new way to enjoy
oatmeal: half a cup of oats, four walnut halves,
        and two tablespoons of Mrs. Butterworth's

low-cal syrup. What a miraculous discovery!
        I dropped twenty pounds worrying the
guilt-ridden scale at Weight Watchers
        until the day our leader asked
the group for their manner of managing
        those cravings we all got around four p.m.

One lady in the back raised her hand.
        "When I get a craving," she chortled,
"I eat a couple of those two-point snacks,
        and that way I never feel depraved!"
That's when I realized the secret of Weight Watchers:
        forget portion control and counting points,

the weight peels off due to uncontrollable
        laughter at such moronic statements.
So I quit and promptly gained back my twenty pounds.
        Now, fat and happy on my two-Diet-Pepsi-
a-day diet, I continue to eat that delicious oatmeal
        with the low-cal syrup and walnuts.

It satisfies now as it did then, and yet
        I still feel depraved!

Acknowledgements

The Broadkill Review: "Leftovers," "Backyard Wisdom—1955"
Catbird Lit: "Four Haiku," "Cleaning Up Cat Puke, Naked, at Seventy," "P.A."
Cathexis Northwest Press: "Les Mouches," "Musée Des Beaux Arts Redux"
The Dope Fiend Daily: "Poet Framed by Snow"
Down in the Dirt: "My Life in Oatmeal"
Eighteen Seventy—Writing from the Fringe: "Degas"
The Ekphrastic Review: "After Day," "Silence"
Flashes: "Blazing Crimson Chirper," "Blue Mind"
Field Guide Poetry Magazine: "Cleaning Up Cat Puke, Naked, at Seventy"
First Literary Review East: "The Truth About Finitude"
Halfway Down The Stairs: "What's Remarkable"
Holiday Café: "Vietnam Again," "Last Laugh," "Waiting Room Again"
I-70 Review: "Slyboots"
Impspired: "A Question," "Credo," "Splainin'," "The Truth About the Universe," "My Face," "Holy Land," "The Truth About Stones," "Mr. Hippie Meets Dr. Responsible"
Infection House: "The Altered Eye," "Prayer in the Time of Coronavirus"
Ink Pantry: "Launched in Light," "St. Rose of Lima," "Requiem in Winter," "The Mirror Stage," "The Sea"
Literary Yard: "Drinks with John," "A Conversation," "New Vows," "The Ventriloquist," and "Sonnet for Camus"
North of Oxford: "In Medias Res"
Orbis: "He Was No Urthona"
Pangolin Review: "The Divine Image"
Raven Cage Zine: "Self-Portrait at Seventy," "A Stitch in Time," "Naked Athene," "The Impossible Profession," "What He Wants," "Towed"
The Raven Review: "Relationship Haiku"
Rusty Truck: "Blackbird"
Sparks of Colliope: "Chagall Room," "COVID Dispatch"
StepAway Magazine: "After COVID is Over"
Sublunary Review: "Congregation Leaving the Reformed Church in Nuenen"
The Sunlight Press: "A Funeral Dance, Walloon Lake, October 2019"
Vox Populi: "Bottled Lives"

"COVID Dispatch" has been nominated for a Pushcart Prize.

"Cleaning Up Cat Puke, Naked, at Seventy" won first place in the 2020 Field Guide Poetry Magazine Poetry Contest

The author would like to thank the following for their support: David Ades, Julie Albright, Suzanna Anderson, Jenny Ashburn, Valerie Bacharach, Monica Beglau, Heath Brougher, Joan E. Bauer, Ace Bogess, Fleda Brown, Jay Carson, Steven Cawte, Dar Charlebois, Diane DeCillis, Sharon Eaks, Angelle Ellis, Robert Fanning, Kerri Finlayson, Corbin and Patti Fowler, Gary Glauber, Hedy Sabbagh Habra, Jodi Haven, Susan and Rich Heeres, Maxine Heller, Jim and Joyce Hutt, Nadia Ibrashi, Jason Irwin, Lori Jareo, Sheila Kelly, Diane Kerr, David Kirby, Larry Kohler, M.L. Liebler and Pam Liebler, Lorette C. Luzajic, Gary Metras, Tayloe McDonald, Ben Pacheco, Nina Padolf, Erin Pierce, Lois Pine, Christine Rhein, Jon Riccio, Bill and Kit Richards, Monica Rico, Jack Ridl, Judith Robinson, Alex Z. Salinas, Janette Schafer, Frank Seeburger, Mother Seraphima, Jan Shoemaker, Sue William Silverman, Wendy and Marty Smith, Artie Solomon, Elizabeth Solsburg, Paul Tayyar, Richard Tillinghast, Matt Ussia, Kevin Walzer, Claire Weiner, Megan Zagorski, and a special thanks to my favorite poet, my wife, Judith A. Brice.

Notes

1 Urthona represented imagination, inspiration, and creativity in William Blake's metaphysical system.

2 See Tuchman, Barbara, *A Distant Mirror*, New York: Random House, 1987.

Made in the USA
Middletown, DE
06 June 2022